Self-Esteem

Effective Strategies For Cultivating Confidence,
Conquering Self-Doubt, Overcoming Shyness, And
Enhancing Self-Esteem

*(The Required Mind-set For Achieving Mastery And
Attaining Genuine Desires In Life)*

Eberhard Rauch

TABLE OF CONTENT

Introduction 1

Recognize That Self-Compassion Does Not Equate To Self-Indulgence. 9

Developing Yourself By Using Your Emotions 26

Speaking With Those You Don't Agree With 50

Find Out How To Stop Having Negative Thoughts. 86

Introduction

Greetings from a stronger, more resilient, and confident version of yourself on your life-changing adventure. The following pages will reveal the keys to realizing your unstoppable potential. This is not simply another book about resilience and self-worth; it's a useful manual full of tried-and-true techniques that will enable you to thrive no matter how chaotic the world gets.

We start our journey by realizing that self-worth is the firm base around our lives. It serves as the cornerstone for our accomplishments, relationships, and goals. If you develop an unwavering sense of self-worth, you'll be ready for anything life throws at you.

Conversely, resilience is the capacity to adjust and prosper in the face of difficulty. With the help of this book, you will be able to improve your mental and emotional toughness and be better able to handle difficult circumstances.

I encourage you to consider your journey and commit to personal transformation as you go through the pages of this book. You'll discover motivational tales, useful activities, and profound insights that can help you develop resilient resilience and unwavering self-worth in all facets of your life.

As you finish reading, remember that while information is powerful, actual change is brought about by action. I respectfully request that you leave a review on Amazon if this book speaks to you and inspires you to begin your journey of self-discovery. Your viewpoint matters and has the power to encourage others to follow their path of steadfastness.

Let's get started on this trip together right now without further ado. Prepare to learn about your own power and how to develop resilience and unwavering self-worth. We are going to set off on an adventure that has the potential to alter your life forever.

Chapter 6: Working Together for Shared Success

Through our exploration of creating and utilizing networks, we realize the enormous potential of teamwork. The third portion explores the mutually beneficial symbiotic dance when people pool their skills to pursue a common objective. Through establishing alliances, collaborations, and cooperative projects, you can increase your influence, use pooled resources, and find creative solutions. The chapter emphasizes that prosperity grows in the rich soil of cooperative efforts rather than solely the product of lone endeavours.

"Building and Leveraging Networks" provides a road map to help you reach your financial goals on the following pages. You discover many opportunities that surpass solo pursuits by appreciating your network, establishing connections with mentors and role models, and adopting a collaborative mindset. As you dig into this chapter, remember that every connection you make, every mentoring you establish, and every team effort you make is a stroke of luck that creates a picture of prosperity and financial success.

The Importance of Your Network in Chapter 6

6.1

The relationships we cultivate provide the cornerstone for our path to wealth growth. We reveal the inherent value of a well-designed network in the first section. We explore the reality that every relationship can provide opportunities for development, wisdom, and growth. Realizing that the calibre of your network directly impacts your life, you set out to create meaningful relationships that improve your financial situation.

Three Steps to Appreciate and Maximize Your Network's Value First Step: Raise Awareness

Start by fostering an understanding of the importance of your network.

Realize that the relationships you cultivate are the foundation of your path to generating wealth. Recognize that every relationship can advance you by providing avenues for development, new insights, and untapped possibilities.

Step 2: Create Insightful Links

Explore the art of purposeful network curation. Seek relationships with people who share your beliefs, ambitions, and goals. Be in the company of people who push you, enlighten you, and provide various perspectives. By carefully selecting your contacts, you build a foundation that improves your financial environment.

Step 3: Encourage Mutual Aid

Recognize that your network's quality is determined by what you contribute and receive. Foster reciprocity by providing your network with advice, ideas, and help. You may turn relationships into cooperative possibilities that accelerate development, enhance your experience, and ultimately help you achieve your financial goals by cultivating a culture of mutual benefit.

Connecting with Mentors and Role Models in Chapter 6 6.2 On our own journey, the knowledge of those who have gone before us acts as a beacon of guidance. In the second part, we look at how to establish a connection with mentors and role models—people who can provide direction, insight, and experience-based advice. We discover the transforming power of hearing from those who have faced comparable difficulties via their stories. You can access a wealth of information by developing these connections, which help you make wise selections and calculated choices.

Three Steps to Establish a Guided Growth Connection with Mentors and Role Models First, choose some role models.

Find people who exemplify the traits and accomplishments you want to emulate first. Look for those who have achieved success by following a similar path. Acknowledge the importance of various role models whose experiences align with your objectives, whether they are in your sector or not.

Step 2: Establish Valuable Relationships

Examine how to establish relationships with mentors and role models.

Be genuinely respectful and curious when interacting with these connections. Make contact to convey your respect for their journey and your desire to absorb their knowledge. A genuine relationship lets in insights and direction that can change your course.

Step 3: Acquire and Utilize Knowledge

After you've made these contacts:

Take an active interest in learning from their experiences.

Pay attention to their tales, take in their counsel, and incorporate their understanding into your path.

Accept their knowledge as a compass to help you avoid mistakes and make wise judgments.

Drawing from their wealth of experience may boost your development and improve your capacity for making wise decisions as you pursue success.

Recognize That Self-Compassion Does Not Equate To Self-Indulgence.

It's critical to understand the distinction between self-indulgence and self-compassion. Self-compassion entails being compassionate, considerate, and understanding toward oneself—especially when facing challenges, setbacks, and suffering. It does not imply abdicating one's responsibilities or clearing oneself of all obligations.

Being harsh and critical of oneself may truly be exhausting and demotivating. People may experience overload and discouragement when continuously criticizing and dwelling on their errors, resulting in burnout and decreased motivation.

On the other hand, self-compassionate individuals are more driven, resilient, and successful in reaching their objectives. People are more likely to overcome failures and persevere in pursuing their objectives when they are kind and empathetic to themselves [20].[21].

Establish modest objectives or participate in self-care practices that enhance mental and physical health. Try rephrasing the negative ideas such that the emphasis is on advancement rather than perfection. You can develop self-compassion and accomplish your goals without losing motivation or drive if you practice and get help.

Write a letter to yourself.

Being aware of your problems and how you speak to yourself about them can help you write a self-compassion letter, which is a very effective method of practising self-compassion. Here is a detailed tutorial on writing one:

Pick a time and location where you won't be bothered. Locate a peaceful, cosy spot where you can concentrate on writing without distractions. Give this exercise at least 20 to 30 minutes.

Do you struggle to find time? If you are a parent, you can encounter it while waiting to pick up your child in the school parking lot. It can be late at night, early in the morning, or as you wait for your charge at the doctor's office if you are a full-time caregiver.

Recognize your suffering and difficulties. Write about your challenges or any pain you are going through in the body of the letter. You might talk about a particular instance or just admit that you're having trouble in general.

Make use of precise instances and circumstances to support your arguments. Rather than stating, "I'm really struggling right now," for instance, you may say, "I've been feeling really anxious and overwhelmed about my workload at work, and I've been beating myself up for not being able to handle it."

Show yourself some empathy. Write as though you were extending this sympathy to a close friend in the following section of the letter. Give yourself grace and empathy. Write with kindness and support. Recognize the difficulties you are facing and provide words of support and encouragement.

Conclude with optimism. Write a concluding note to yourself that is encouraging and reassuring. Saying something like, "I believe in myself and my ability to handle this situation with kindness and resilience," is one example of what you could say.

Aloud read the letter. After completing the letter, read it out loud to yourself. Allow the words to truly settle in by taking your time. It might even be something you want to read again in a few days or save somewhere you can refer to again.

Above all, practice self-compassion. It takes effort to write a self-compassion letter, and at first, it could feel awkward or uncomfortable. However, it can be an effective strategy for lowering self-criticism and increasing self-compassion with time and practice.

Make Affirmations Yourself-Kindness Practice

Repetition of positive sentences or phrases, known as affirmations, helps to foster self-improvement and optimistic thinking. They can be applied to lessen negative self-talk, develop a positive outlook, and increase self-confidence. Affirmations assist in focusing the mind on good feelings and ideas, which makes them an effective technique for developing gratitude. Here's how to carry them out:

Select affirmations that speak to you personally. List a few uplifting phrases or affirmations that bring forth thoughts of compassion and encouragement. As an illustration:

● I believe in my wisdom and intuition to guide me.● I am worthy of love and compassion, just as I am.● I am free to make errors and learn from them.

I am deserving of self-care and taking the time to nurture myself. I am not defined by my mistakes or failures but by my resilience and compassion. I am grateful for my journey and all that I have learned. I am strong and capable, even in the face of difficulty from myself and others. I am doing the best I can, and that is enough.

Put them in writing. Place your affirmations in a visible spot for easy access by writing them down in a journal or on a sticky note. This will remind you to say them aloud throughout the day.

Every day, repeat the affirmations. Decide on a designated time to recite your affirmations, such as before bed or first thing in the morning. You can say each affirmation aloud or in silence to yourself multiple times. As you say each one, allow yourself to experience warmth and comfort.

Throughout the day, cultivate self-compassion and thankfulness. When you begin to feel nervous or irritated, remember your affirmations. They can also be incorporated into the self-compassion breaks and the loving-kindness meditation we will discuss soon. Give some thought to the little pleasures in life, like a steaming cup of tea or a stunning sunset.

You can lessen your self-criticism and develop self-compassion by using these affirmations. You start to change your perspective and adopt a more understanding and encouraging attitude toward yourself when you consistently repeat them.

Meditate in a loving-kindness manner.

Reducing stress and blood pressure are two of meditation's many mental and physical health advantages [23]. Did you know it can make you feel more connected, self-kind, and mindful? In addition to the benefits listed above, a loving-kindness meditation offers the opportunity to cultivate human connection and present-moment mindfulness. This is a detailed instruction manual for doing loving-kindness meditation:

Select a spot. Locate a peaceful, comfortable area where you won't be bothered for a few minutes.

Decide on an objective. Set a goal for yourself before you start. One possible statement would be, "I want to cultivate feelings of love and kindness toward myself and others."

Pay attention to your breathing. Shut your eyes and inhale deeply many times. Next, focus on your breathing and pay attention to the sensations it makes as it enters and exits your body.

Recite the words. Start saying loving-kindness affirmations to yourself. Say something like, "May I be happy, may I be healthy, may I be safe, may I be at peace." Let the words soak in by slowly and deliberately repeating these phrases.

Enlarge the compassionate circle. After repeating the lines to yourself for a few minutes, you can extend your compassion to others. You might begin by repeating the sentences to a loved one, like a family member or acquaintance. Afterwards, you can widen the circle to include strangers, friends, and challenging individuals.

Develop a loving and compassionate attitude. You can concentrate on the physical sensations of warmth and relaxation in your body or visualize a warm, shining light in your chest.

Put an end to your meditation. You can conclude the meditation by taking a few deep breaths whenever ready. Wait until you are ready to wake up and face the remainder of the day.

One of the most effective ways to develop love, kindness, and compassion for yourself and others is through loving-kindness meditation. Try to use it once a few days, at the very least, to help you refocus your thoughts more constructively.

MANAGING YOUR TIME THOUGHTFULLY AND WISELY

Teenagers often have so many responsibilities that anxiety and tension can rapidly become the norm for them if they have little to no control over their time. According to the school, you have to attend dozens of classes, turn in homework, participate in extracurricular activities, and hang out with pals. Along with participating in family gatherings and everyday activities at home, you could also have to complete several duties. Dealing with everything that is required of you can be incredibly draining. For this reason, making sensible use of the 24 hours a day will spare you a great deal of needless hassle. Good-time managers gain a great deal of advantages. The following list provides instances of how managing your time well can greatly simplify and improve your quality of life:

You feel more confident doing things because you've done a lot of planning ahead.

You experience a significant reduction in tension and anxiety.

You are more poised and capable of handling shifting circumstances.

You overcome obstacles more quickly and skillfully.

Effective time management enables you to finish your work on time and regularly engage in activities you enjoy.

It increases your chances of trying new things and growing as a person.

You'll likely do exceptionally well in school and extracurricular activities.

Since you have to remain up late to meet deadlines that are drawing near, you won't experience sleep deficiency issues.

You get brighter and healthier. You have time to engage in energizing activities like yoga and meditation and good habits like eating well and exercising.

You can dedicate more time to your connections.

Your daily output has increased, and you have more opportunities to broaden your success.

You develop into a more capable and dependable team member.

Fantastic advice on how to completely transform your time management is provided here. Let's examine some of the routines you adopt to improve your effectiveness as a personal time manager:

Organizing your day in advance, ideally the night before, should always come first. Doing this can save time pondering what to do when and be more productive the next day.

Keep a little notepad to jot down your daily objectives and to-do lists. You can record your plans on your phone if you don't prefer to use a paper notepad. You can use a variety of applications as a daily planner. Visit the Play Store or your App Store to check them out. Look through them all and select the most convenient for you.

Make use of calendar alerts on Google. You may plan and keep your daily objectives in order using a digital phone calendar.

Become comfortable with saying "No." We are surrounded by countless distractions every day. You can better manage your time if you practice self-control and discipline. The purpose of social media apps is to entice you to spend a lot of time using them. The desire to spend hours in front of a screen can be difficult to resist, yet it is a goal that can be attained.

Adopting discipline is difficult. But the more you practice, the more natural it will become for you to manage your time well.

Utilize your timer or alarm to set the appropriate duration for each task you plan. You will feel more urgency when you know how little time you have left to finish a task.

Establish and preserve a neat, orderly, and clean atmosphere. Have you ever been late for school or an errand because you couldn't remember where you put something? Isn't it disappointing and incredibly frustrating? Without even the slightest doubt, the answer is definitely yes. It may wind up hurrying your entire day and wasting time. Your brain will quickly recognize where things are and assist you in remembering where they are if you ensure everything is in its designated spot. With this easy habit, you may complete more tasks on your daily to-do list and save time.

Schedule your most challenging work for when you are most productive. Pay attention to when you are most productive. The temptation to put things off is constant when they're tough. Plan your errands to be finished during the first few hours of the day when you are the most alert and energized to avoid putting them off. You'll be less anxious and able to do those duties more successfully.

Assign a specific amount of time to each modest, achievable job that needs to be completed. When a task is not broken down into manageable pieces, it might seem overwhelming and deter you from beginning. Therefore, you must take your time determining what you can accomplish on a given day and what may wait until the next day. Assigning some of your work to people who might be willing and able to assist you is another strategy to help you do this.

Begin your day as early as possible, preferably at the same time each day. Getting an early start to your day allows you to accomplish more before midday. However, if you are not a morning person, you may have found that you require assistance doing the remaining tasks for the day. Making the most of the chances that arise in the early hours is beneficial. It may seem hard to break the habit of staying up late, but it's rather simple. Many alarms will help you stay awake even if you are inclined to disregard one. This way, the other alarms will still force you to wake up. To wake up and prepare your body for the day, you can also go for an early morning jog or any other workout you enjoy. Your body will become accustomed to waking up at that precise hour, so the more regularly you exercise and stick to this schedule, the less you will even need the alarms.

If you want to be a great achiever, get eight hours of sleep every night. Sleep is essential. Conversely, sleeping too much causes your body to become less functional and unable to function as well as it once could. Have you ever noticed that sleeping too much causes you to feel more exhausted than energized? Your body tells you that getting too much sleep is not a good idea. Dreams come true while you are awake and actively seeking them; they do not come true while asleep. Your body will grow accustomed to your regular sleeping schedule as you cultivate disciplined sleeping habits, and anything outside of it will seem strange and unsettling to you. You may teach your body to adapt to the best practice for you.

There's no limit to what you can accomplish once you take charge of your time. Use extreme caution while managing your time. Spend some time at the end of each week analyzing how you used the 168 hours available. The more you examine your time management pattern, the more you'll be able to pinpoint areas for improvement the next week so that you may use your time more wisely than before.

Developing Yourself By Using Your Emotions

Both advantages and disadvantages are present. However, one thing is certain: emotions are a necessary part of our existence. A small amount of emotion can occasionally be beneficial; therefore, emotions are not always negative. It prevents us from acting insensitively and uncaringly while making decisions. It pushes us to take action and look for answers. It isn't until these decisions entail excessive emotion that they become problematic.

All people have emotions, even if everyone experiences them differently. Despite this, everyone can agree that emotions are strong forces. We must finally learn how to master them since they are really powerful. The next few chapters will concentrate on being emotionally mature—thinking, making wise decisions, and maintaining composure under pressure. To develop the ability to take charge of your situation and remain in control no matter what.

It will be necessary to make some big changes in several areas to learn how to control your emotions. It's uncommon that change is simple, particularly when it involves aspects of your personality. One of the biggest obstacles in your quest to become the master of your emotions will be trying to break free from negative emotional habits that have been a part of your life for so long that you don't know any other way to handle them (like learning to control your anger, for example).

Although these adjustments won't be simple, they will be worthwhile. Gaining control of your emotions can lead to a better quality of life. A happier life for you and the ones you care about as well. There will always be emotional triggers since you are not alone. You're always in social situations and have to deal with people continuously. It will undoubtedly occur occasionally. These triggers might occasionally be uncontrollable. Your emotions and how you react to your triggers are the only things under your control. It is up to you to decide whether or not to make a conscious attempt to alter your feelings.

Fight the want to rise to the occasion and give in to the temptation of reacting to whatever is agitating you since the force of these emotions is so great within you. It will be challenging because you must consciously urge yourself to react differently, going against your initial, automatic reaction. To respond more effectively.

How to Rewire Your Brain to Think Positively

You can start managing your thoughts so they go in the opposite direction if your mind is already capable of complaining and being negative without you even having to think about it. There are numerous advantages to adopting a more optimistic outlook on life. It improves you and enables you to discover the bright side of any circumstance you encounter. It gives you the freedom to be yourself without being controlled by bitterness, melancholy, envy, anxiety, or any other unfavourable feeling that may have previously held you back.

You must go on this emotional mastery path, which includes rewiring your mind for the better. Start by taking the initial actions listed below:

Complete What You Started: You must support your prefrontal cortex with planning exercises to build your mind for positive thinking. For instance, when you're tired but must finish a report for the approaching deadline. Making a plan will help you get over this lack of desire. You can treat yourself to worry-free, undisturbed sleep if you complete your work; otherwise, you'll have to do much more work in a shorter period. Your brain is trained to believe in and strive for your anticipated future and that it will finally arrive when you complete your chores and treat yourself afterwards.

Acknowledge that rejection is a part of life and learn to be okay with it. You may encounter rejection occasionally, but things will go your way other times. What matters is how you respond to the latter. Putting things into perspective will help you learn to accept rejection. Consider it a momentary setback that is likely preparing you for an even better chance down the road rather than viewing it as a failure. You may have gone through this multiple times before, and you don't need to change the way you think about rejection. Rewire it for a new way of thinking.

Encourage Your Emotional Styles: You can foster an atmosphere that encourages your emotions by becoming more conscious of your own. At that point, you can adjust your way of living and daily activities to support these emotional patterns rather than rejecting or allowing them to spiral out of control. One method to learn how to control your emotions is to support them. They are an integral part of who you are, and attempting to ignore or fight them will make it more difficult for you to learn how to deal with them.

Let Go of anger: When you decide to cling to your grievances and anger, the only person you are punishing is yourself. By deciding to hold onto this negative feeling, you are depriving yourself of any happiness at all. The resentment that you hold onto will only make you feel bad. You'll waste time blaming other people for your unfortunate situation when, in reality, you should only be held accountable for your decision to cling to this feeling. You want to be happy, so learn to let it go.

Consider "How Can This Assist?- Regardless of how dire things appear, there's always a bright side; all you have to do is look for it by asking yourself the appropriate questions. The last thing you may be considering after suffering a setback is how this circumstance may benefit you. No matter how hopeless or bad the circumstances are, you can train your mind to think positively and keep your optimism by considering what. Think about what you've learned from this experience. What can I do going ahead to improve it? What good lesson can you learn from this experience? You can choose how many lessons you want to learn—one, two, or more.

Birds of a Positive Feather Flock Together: It may be time to consider adjusting your immediate social group if you've been trapped in a negative cycle for far too long. Which members of your family and circle of acquaintances are generally cheerful and have an optimistic view of life? You should start spending more time with these people. You will only feel burdened by negative people. They will deplete your vitality and become an unnecessary mental and emotional strain. When you are in the company of positive thinkers, you will gradually change how you think to reflect their perspective and insight. If you cannot completely remove the unpleasant individuals from your life, limit the time you spend with them.

Speak Positively to Yourself: Everyone discusses with themselves, but since these conversations occur privately, no one else is aware of them. Are you being kind to yourself when you do talk to yourself? Do you tell yourself, "I can do anything I set my mind to, and I am stronger than I believe"?

Do your chats with yourself seem more like I'm not good enough, can't do this, and I'll never be good enough?

Your thoughts can impact things positively as well as negatively. See the negative thoughts you are thinking as rocks in front of you that you must physically move to make room in your head for better, more positive ideas. You must force every self-defeating notion out of your head and begin thinking only good thoughts. As soon as you think something negative, stop and immediately replace it with something positive.

Say aloud and with a smile at least one thing for which you are thankful as soon as you wake up. Even if you may not always feel enthusiastic, make it a practice to wake up with energy and enthusiasm.

However, you may drive enthusiasm out of yourself until it manifests. The well-known self-improvement trainer Dale Carnegie once told us, "You will B.E. enthusiastic when you ACT like you are enthusiastic."

Once you concentrate entirely on the positive aspects of your life, no matter how minor they may seem, this is surprisingly simple to achieve. You are more fortunate than you know if you can list five things in your life for which you are instantly thankful. It's time to begin listing all the things you should be thankful for and utilize those reasons to greet each morning with a smile and a positive attitude.

Quit Assuming the Worst: Recall all the times you've envisioned the worst-case situations occurring. How many of those possibilities were true based on your assumptions?

Should they not, then consider why you are incessantly supposing the worst will happen to you. That's the issue, and now that you understand that you are your own worst enemy, it's time to rewire your brain to break the habit of assuming the worst.

Decide to focus on realizing that the things you picture are only your imagination rather than trying to convince yourself that the worst conceivable things will happen to you.

Pay It Forward: There's no better way to create a perpetually positive and happy loop than by paying it forward. Paying it forward, for those who are unfamiliar, is the idea of returning the favour by showing compassion to others. The joy you get from a simple act of generosity motivates you to want to do something nice for someone else, like when you're at the drive-through and realize the stranger in the car in front of you just paid for your lunch. Your deed of kindness will then encourage them to do the same for others, and so on. You increase someone else's pleasure and your own when you truly make them feel wonderful without asking for anything in return. Sometimes, the tiniest deed can make the biggest impact on someone else.

In the larger scheme of things, buying a homeless person lunch might not seem like a huge deal, but for that one homeless person, your act of kindness might be the best thing they have seen all day. Take it upon yourself to initiate the pay-it-forward cycle rather than waiting for someone else to do so.

Section 7

Giving Up on Compassion

Disengaging with compassion is extremely important in the context of escaping codependency and forming healthier relationships. Codependents frequently become involved in relationships that endanger their emotional health. Disengaging with compassion is crucial to letting go of codependent behaviours, accepting emotional freedom, and fostering relationships based on well-being.

Significance of disengaging with empathy, talking about the difficulties of saying goodbye and offering a doable step for creating a disengagement plan.

Releasing Dangerous Connections

For those who are deeply ingrained in codependency, ending harmful relationships can be one of the most difficult yet freeing experiences. These partnerships frequently involve components like addiction, abuse, deception, or a persistent imbalance in the support system exchange. Disengaging from connections that require empathy and kindness is part of disengaging with compassion. Disengaging with compassion is based on several fundamental principles:

1. Acceptance: Realizing that you have no power over or influence over another person's actions or decisions is the first step toward disengaging.

2. Boundaries: While navigating the disengagement process, respect your boundaries and voice your requirements. Your boundaries serve as your protectors when it comes to your health.

3. Self-Care: As you remove yourself from the connection, prioritize self-care and self-compassion. Consult with loved ones, friends, or licensed therapists for assistance.

4. Letting Go of Resentment: Letting go of anger and resentment is a prerequisite to acting compassionately. Holding onto bad feelings can only make your pain worse.

5. Setting Your Well-Being as a Priority: Shift your focus from the other person's actions to your well-being. Try to look after your mental, emotional, and physical well-being.

6. Retain compassion and empathy for the person you are ending your relationship with. Recognize that the unfavourable dynamics of

the relationship may have been influenced by their problems or struggles.

7. Emotional Disengagement: One of the most important aspects of disengaging from compassion is emotional detachment. This is releasing yourself from emotional entanglement rather than turning aloof or disinterested.

Handling Loss and Separation

Loss and separation are natural byproducts of turning away from compassion. Even when it is acknowledged that ending an unhealthy relationship is necessary, doing so can be extremely difficult emotionally. A crucial step in the disengagement process is handling these feelings well:

1. Handling the Grief: Recognize that, regardless of how toxic the relationship was, it is normal to feel grief at the end of it. Give yourself permission to face and work through your pain without feeling guilty about it.

2. Looking for a Support System: Broaden your search for a support system, which could include friends, relatives, or licensed therapists. During this time, it can be really helpful to share your feelings and experiences.

3. Keeping a Journal: Consider whether you could keep a journal in which you could write your feelings, ideas, and reflections on ending the relationship. Expressing yourself through writing can be a healing process.

4. Stressing Self-Care: Place emphasis on caring for your physical and emotional needs. Engage in pursuits that promote your health and aid in your recovery.

5. The Practice of Mindfulness: When faced with emotional turmoil, mindfulness practices can help keep you centred and in the moment. Deep breathing exercises and meditation might be especially beneficial.

6. Avoiding Isolation: While introspection and recovery are important, avoid becoming overly

solitary. To prevent loneliness, stay in touch with encouraging friends and family.

7. Celebrating Personal Development: Recognize that ending a toxic relationship presents a chance for introspection and personal growth. Keep your focus on your path to recovery and personal growth.

Developing a Plan for Disengagement: An Actionable Step

Making a disengagement strategy might provide a systematic way to separate from harmful relationships while maintaining respect and love. The following stages can help you create a disengagement plan:

1. Examine the Relationship: Get a thorough grasp of the particular issues and dynamics that make the relationship problematic by carefully examining it.

2. Set Clear and Firm Boundaries: Defining clear and firm boundaries is essential to ensuring your safety in the connection.

3. Communicate Your Intent: When you're ready, have an open and understanding conversation regarding your choice to step away from the other person. Make sure to make your expectations and boundaries clear.

4. Seek Assistance: Throughout the disengagement process, seek the assistance of friends, family, or licensed therapists who can offer emotional support and direction.

5. Create a Support System: Find people who can help you through the disengagement process, provide advice, or just listen to you with compassion.

6. Formulate a Self-Care strategy: Formulate a self-care plan to put your health first during disengagement. Activities that make you happy, relaxed, and emotionally nourished may fall under this category.

7. Disengagement as a Daily Practice: Maintain your limits and put your health first as you

consistently engage in disengagement. Recall that the process of disengaging is continuous.

8. Enjoy Your Progress: As you move through the disengagement process, acknowledge and appreciate each new growth phase. Acknowledge your tenacity and resolve.

Giving up compassion is a deep and liberating journey. It gives you the capacity to break free from codependent tendencies, find who you are, and build better relationships going forward. It is a journey of self-discovery and healing that may eventually result in a happier and more contented existence.

DIVIDE SELF

Though I often emphasize the value of listening, you participate actively in the conversation. You might even spend more time striking up small talk than a reserved friend to move the conversation along. When engaging in active listening with others, you must be able to share as much as your communication partners.

Additionally, you'll constantly be questioned by others.

You could want to be the star, to leave others in amazement of your social skills, but if you're like me when I started learning social skills, you're probably thinking, "I need a talk aid. It's quick to listen. I don't need to listen to help." Yes, neither the lead guitarist nor the singer are really good conversationalists. The event planner has combined their roles as stage manager and master of ceremonies into one person. For them, being the star is not the goal. It's about selecting the subject, being inclusive, enhancing the atmosphere, and motivating their finest performers.

People appreciate you even if it might sound unglamorous to lean into a conversation, clasp hands, listen closely, and ask, "Tell me all about how sheep have changed your life." When you are attentively listening, there are a few beneficial ideas you can keep in mind.

Show consideration for others.

Give up thinking about yourself. It may sound strange, but you ignore other people mainly when you're preoccupied with yourself.

Be tolerant and nonjudgmental: Man experiencing self-doubt over hitting a girl while doing drug tests? Alright, don't voice any disagreements. Recall that this is the moment for a gold narrative if you encounter someone like this. Savour everything and respect their experience because you could never have anything similar.

Never minimize others. If someone presents a problem or idea that you believe can be solved quickly or is trivial in comparison to your viewpoint, you should take a step back and decide to treat it seriously. You won't believe how important this problem is.

Clarify any unclear or conflicting statements made. Occasionally, you just want to move on from a conversation that doesn't make sense to you. You want to know more when you're paying attention intentionally. It's obvious you care by doing this. It's also worth noting that occasionally, a story that was purposefully left unclear due to its risky existence turns out to be gold once more.

Engage with emotional threads: Assume you can follow an emotional and rational stream on any topic. Keep strands in mind. You might discuss the type of school someone was attending, the calibre of their courses, or just what it was like to study there. The latter is far more pertinent to good active listening. Examine these suggestions before engaging in any social setting and discover how often you or those around you may connect to them!

Effective communication is beneficial in any kind of relationship. Both personal and professional interactions are involved. Your communication abilities will significantly improve if you can cultivate active listening.

The first half of any encounter is being heard. Please do yourself a favour and concentrate on your capacity for active listening. It can greatly affect how well you succeed at work and in your intimate relationships.

3.4 Talking Like a Pro

Welcome to the human world. A couple of tigers in a clearing through the jungle chance glance at one another. Tigers in the forest slightly differ from urban straight animals in the corporate jungle (also known as jungle singles or social jungle). They make the instinctual decision, "If our gazing hisses — came to scratch — came to claw — who would win? Does one of us possess stronger survival abilities?" By interacting with and observing one another, humans carry on the cycle. When laughing and uttering, "How are you doing?" Hello," "Howdy," or "Hey," they naturally, immediately and quickly size each other up like tigers. They don't measure the length or sharpness of each other's claws. As they have described, they judge each other on a tool that is more important to survival. Human beings judge the interpersonal abilities of one another. While they may not know the names of the specific studies to prove it, they feel the truth: 85 per cent of one's lifetime performance is directly due to communication skills. They do not get to know the U.S. employers select candidates with good communication skills and attitudes above schooling, experience, and training. But they know communication skills are getting people to the top. Therefore, carefully watching each other during a casual conversation makes it almost instantly evident who the bigger cat is in the human jungle. It doesn't take long for people to know who a person of "importance" is. One cliché, one disrespectful comment, one over-anxious. May lose a relationship or business connection, which is potentially significant. One dumb move and the corporate or social ladder will tumble down. The methods in this section should help make sure you're making all the right moves so it doesn't happen. The following communication skills provide you with a leg to continue your climb to the top of any ladder you choose.

Speaking With Those You Don't Agree With

Talking with those you don't always agree with has significance. Your viewpoint on a topic may change. You could provide evidence to back up your disagreement. During the talk, you can learn something new about your partner. And that kind of engagement may be engaging when we esteem each other and behave like adults.
But perhaps reverence gets in the way too often, and we start acting more like our five-

year-old selves than the collected, collected grownups we might all be.

Especially with family, spouses, and close friends, we frequently need to have difficult conversations about matters we disagree on to come to answers.

Discuss topics such as damaged sentiments experienced by others or divergent opinions about how two partners should allocate their finances. "The price tag of not having the conversation is high." That is to say, even while there isn't a disagreement that requires resolution, the consequences of skipping these kinds of discussions could still be significant.

You'll grasp the topic better if you talk to a friend you disagree with about whether faith should be taught in schools or if a single-payer healthcare system is more prudent. It fortifies your position by making it more evident why your beliefs hold up in the face of opposing viewpoints.

Here's how to disagree graciously.

The skills required to have meaningful conversations about income taxes are pretty much the same whether you disagree with your wife about raising your first child or with a friend of a friend you met at a dinner party.

It's not a result of the disparities in competencies. They feel so different from one another because of the emotional load they carry in different ways. This is the alternative approach she and others want to take.

Never presume malice

It almost always deters us from fully understanding and believing what someone is doing when we assume they have bad intentions. We forget that we are stuck in the initial wave of frustration and that the discourse will never be able to go over it because they are human people with lifetime experiences that have shaped their thoughts.

Yet, when we assume a neutral or positive aim, we provide our thoughts with a much more robust dialogue structure.

Remain impartial.

Keep the talk productive right from the start. Ask questions that show you understand the context of a situation without coming across as arrogant, especially if you are inquiring about the other person's point of view. Furthermore, it's not surprising that you accept condescending with such hesitancy. You want to begin from a neutral point where no one prods the other person's feelings with a stick (or asks them to).

By asking questions, we can help others understand the differences between our ideas when approaching them along political lines. This is important because it allows the opposing side to highlight contradictions in our positions if we don't know where they originated. We are not capable of winning arguments.

However, there is a reason to ask questions; it lets someone know they are understood. You mimicked your friends almost quickly after they stopped asking you stupid questions on Twitter and started criticizing you instead. You had room to talk because of their questions, but they should urge you to ask them questions and pay close attention to their responses. It changed the dynamics of communication drastically.

Chapter 2: Seizing the Opportunity for Change: Embracing the Present's Power

Against the warm walls of a shabby little Italian café, Giorgio busied himself with a slightly bent letter and an unfinished shot of espresso. The calm of his afternoon was disturbed by an intruder from his past, sent by his brother who had vanished long ago in Milan. Pencils on the paper pulled him more and farther into the past, igniting ancient feuds within the family and bringing back memories of a carefree past. Time seemed to be folding in on itself, warping his present reality and bringing memories of the past into the present.

His thoughts were filled with vivid memories of home, including sun-drenched vineyards tucked away on Tuscan hills, boots covered in mud from football games played in the rain, and lighthearted banter that quickly turned into sour arguments. Each memory cast a shadow of regret and longing, drawing him more into the frigid depths of the past and away from the cosy confines of the café. He knew his present was becoming less colourful due to these links to his past. He began to yearn to escape these regret-bound confines and fully experience the meaning of his current life.

Through the mist-veiled window, Giorgio looked out into Florence's cobblestone streets, the sound of children laughing setting the scene for a typical lazy afternoon. An instinctive part of him wanted to disappear into their world, suffocate in their contagious presentness, let go of the past, and smother any fears about the future before they could form. The smell of roasted beans mingled with his thoughts as he sat there, lost in meditation, guiding him gradually towards the transformational power of the present.

He released his hold on the tattered letter as it fell to the worn, uneven table, leaning closer to a conclusion. His mind paused between his unknown future and his past mistakes. It was difficult, but just as a focused sculptor worked tirelessly to create his work, Giorgio started to shape his life in the here and now. Gradually, the cacophony of his recollections and worries about the future began to subside, to be replaced by the life that was happening in front of him. The lively banter between him and the barista and the infrequent rain tapping on the café's windows all felt distinct, genuine, and alive.

His anxieties and remorse had become faraway murmurs, like inmates in a different realm. Giorgio was struck with a sudden and powerful realization about the importance of living in the now, its ability to shape his future, and its ability to set him free from the chains of his past. A powerful question persisted as the moments blended with the pleasant scent of the café: Isn't it more satisfying to enjoy the vividness of the present rather than let the ghosts of the past or the dancing shadows of the future ensnare us?

By releasing the power of the present, we can transcend time and enter a place where miracles are possible. Each breath and step we take turns into a holy act of creation. We can control our thoughts and feelings, create the reality we live in, and feel the deep joy of being alive.

However, how can we start embracing the power of the here and now? The first step is mindfulness, which is the discipline of being conscious. We can learn to notice our thoughts objectively and to change our attention from the past or the future to the present moment by practising mindfulness.

Meditation is one method of developing mindfulness. We can train our minds to let go of distractions and become fully present by sitting still and focusing on the here and now. This has nothing to do with attaining some unattainable goal or state of perfection. Instead, it is about continually bringing our thoughts back to the breath or a selected focal point and bringing our attention back to the present moment whenever our thoughts stray.

Start the process of rewiring our brains and thinking differently. We can improve our capacity for staying in the present and change our attention from regrets and anxieties to the beauty and possibilities of the here.

We can make a new reality for ourselves by embracing the power of the present. We can let go of our worries and burdens from the past and present and enter a realm of boundless opportunities. Life happens here, miracles happen, and we can bring our desires to pass in the present moment. So why hold off? Together, we can seize the opportunity to live fully in the now and set out on a path towards personal development.

Living in the present is one of the most important practices for personal development and transformation. A new reality can arise when we let go of our past regrets and anxieties about the future. In this part, we will explore various techniques that can help us let go of future worries and past sorrows, allowing us to fully embrace the power of the present.

Mindfulness meditation is one method that may be useful in easing future anxiety. We become conscious of our thoughts and feelings without passing judgment on them when we direct our attention to the here and now. This practice teaches us to be more at peace and gain a more impartial outlook on life. We can learn to anchor ourselves in the present moment and let go of worries about the future by practising meditation regularly.

The exercise of gratitude is another effective strategy. Through refocusing our attention from our shortcomings to our blessings, we can develop an attitude of plenty and satisfaction. Having gratitude in our lives makes the present moment more meaningful and gives us a sense of joy and fulfilment. Release the need to constantly worry about the future.

Although it can be difficult, moving past regrets is essential for personal development. Forgiveness—both of oneself and others—is a useful tool. By forgiving ourselves for past mistakes and forgiving others for any harm they may have caused, we free ourselves from the burdens of resentment and guilt. This act of forgiveness allows us to heal and create space for new experiences and opportunities.

Self-reflection is another powerful tool for releasing past regrets. It is important to approach this process with compassion and without judgment. Instead of dwelling on past mistakes, we can use them as valuable learning opportunities and consciously decide to move forward with a renewed sense of purpose.

In summary, releasing future anxieties and past regrets is crucial for embracing the power of the present. Techniques such as mindfulness meditation, gratitude, forgiveness, and self-reflection can help us let go of worries about the future and regrets about the past. Living in the present moment creates space for personal growth and transformation, allowing us to tap into the joy, love, and success already within us. The journey requires commitment and practice, but the rewards are well worth it. So, let us embark on this transformative journey together, embracing the power of the present and creating a new reality for ourselves.

Discovering how to reset your mind in the present is the key to personal growth and transformation. The power of the present moment lies in its ability to free us from the shackles of the past and the anxieties of the future. When we learn to fully embrace and live in the present, we open ourselves up to a new reality filled with joy, love, and success.

In this moment, there is no past, no future, only the pure and unfiltered experience of the present. It is in this space that true transformation can occur.

We often find ourselves caught up in the busyness of life, constantly worrying about what tomorrow holds or regretting mistakes from the past. This constant state of mental time travel keeps us from fully experiencing the richness of the present moment. But it doesn't have to be this way.

Chapter 4: Negotiating in Different Contexts

1. In Business: Contracts, Salaries, Partnerships

T

The business realm, with its diverse landscapes, offers a myriad of negotiation scenarios. Whether it's hashing out contract terms, discussing a potential raise, or forging a new partnership, each context demands unique strategies and nuances. This section delves into these business-centric negotiations, shedding light on their intricacies and offering insights for effective and mutually beneficial outcomes.

1.1. Contracts: Crafting the Blueprint

Contracts, the backbone of business operations, are intricate agreements defining terms, conditions, obligations, and expectations.

Negotiating them requires a delicate balance of firmness and flexibility.

- Know Your Non-Negotiables: Identify the terms you absolutely cannot compromise on before entering discussions.

-Research and Preparation: Understand market standards, competitor clauses, and potential legal implications.

- Focus on Clarity: Ensure all terms are explicit, minimizing ambiguity or potential loopholes.

-Seek Win-Win: While protecting your interests, identify areas where concessions won't hurt but can offer significant value to the other party.

1.2. Salaries: The Delicate Dance of Worth

Salary negotiations are deeply personal, often intertwined with one's sense of value and worth. They require tact, transparency, and a clear understanding of market trends.

- Benchmarking: Research industry salary standards for the specific role, location, and experience level.
- Quantify Your Value: Come prepared with tangible achievements, metrics, or contributions that justify your requested compensation.
- Consider Total Compensation: Look beyond just the base salary.
- Practice Empathy: Understand the employer's constraints and perspectives. This not only helps in negotiations but also fosters goodwill.

1.3. Partnerships: Navigating Shared Ventures

Partnerships between businesses or individuals involve a confluence of visions, goals, and resources. They demand a holistic approach, emphasizing mutual growth and shared success.

- Shared Vision and Values: Before diving into specifics, ensure alignment in overarching goals and principles.

-Define Roles and Responsibilities: Clearly outline who brings what to the table and the expectations from each party.

-Discuss Exit Strategies: It might seem pessimistic, but discussing potential dissolution terms can prevent complications later.

- Cultural and Organizational Synergy: In cross-company partnerships, understand and respect the organizational cultures, ensuring they can coexist harmoniously.

With their vast scope and varied contexts, business negotiations are intricate dances of strategy, understanding, and foresight. Whether delineating a contract's fine print, advocating for one's financial worth, or envisioning a shared entrepreneurial journey, success lies in preparation, empathy, and the unwavering pursuit of mutual benefit. As we journey through the business world, these negotiations sculpt the path, turning challenges into opportunities and visions into tangible realities.

2. In Personal Life: Navigating Intimate Arenas

While the business world offers structured negotiation settings, personal life presents deeply nuanced and emotionally charged scenarios. Here, negotiations are less about transactions and more about relationships, understanding, and mutual respect. Let's dissect these personal arenas of negotiation, highlighting their unique challenges and offering strategies for harmonious resolutions.

2.1. Purchases: Beyond Price Tags

Personal purchases, from homes to cars to gadgets, are intertwined with aspirations, needs, and emotional factors.

-Research is Key: Before negotiating a purchase, understand the market value, reviews, and alternatives. This arms you with information to discuss prices and quality.

-Determine Your Budget: Know your financial constraints. This will help you negotiate within limits and avoid impulsive overspending.

-Emotion vs. Logic: While emotional factors like aesthetics or brand loyalty play a role, base your final decisions on logical considerations such as utility, durability, and value for money.

-Willingness to Walk Away: Sometimes, the best negotiation tactic in personal purchases is the willingness to explore other options if terms don't align.

2.2. Relationships: The Heart's Negotiations

Relationship negotiations are delicate, involving feelings, expectations, and vulnerabilities.

-Open Communication: Encourage honest conversations about needs, boundaries, and aspirations. This fosters mutual understanding.

-Active Listening: In relationship discussions, listening is as crucial as speaking. It validates feelings and ensures both parties feel heard.

- Compromise with Care: While compromising is essential, ensure it doesn't lead to resentment or feeling undervalued.
- Seek Counseling: For persistent disagreements, consider relationship counselling.

2.3. Resolving Family Disputes: Treading with Tenderness

Family presents unique negotiation challenges with its intricate web of history, emotions, and connections.

- Stay Calm and Objective: In heated family disagreements, strive to stay calm. Avoid dredging up unrelated past grievances.
- Define the Core Issue: Pinpoint the primary cause of disagreement. This prevents discussions from becoming overly broad or convoluted.
- Prioritize Relationship Over Victory: Winning an argument but straining a family relationship

might not be a worthy trade-off. Seek solutions that maintain familial bonds.

-Involve a Mediator: A mediator or family therapist can provide structured resolution pathways in complex family disputes, especially involving assets or legacies.

Section 9 - Powerful body language

"The viewers won't get the right word unless they see the right picture. We believe it when we see it."

"Winning Body Language" by Mark Bowden.

You can dress the part and say the right things, which are both very important, but if your body language doesn't match or go with what you're saying and how you look, people won't believe you. In other words, you won't be able to get your point across effectively.

As you walk in the door, your body tells people everything they need to know about you. Body language is the quickest way to show confidence and make a good first impression.

Because we're always looking for people who can lead us. Carnegie Mellon conducted a large study that found that a professional's confidence is more important than their image, skills, or background.

Body language, or "body talk," tells people more than half what they need to know about how you feel about them. In fact, 55 per cent of a message is sent through body language, 38 per cent through the tone of voice, and only 7 per cent through the words themselves. Yes, 93% of conversation is done without words.

Stand tall and keep your stance wide.

When you stand up straight, people know immediately that you have something to say and are confident. Stand like a winner. You'll not only look more sure of yourself, but you'll also feel more sure of yourself. And remember that if you look confident, people will think you have something to be confident about. People take what you show them,

Also, when you're sitting, you should keep your back straight. Dr Lillian Glass, a body language expert, says that slouching or bad posture sends the message that you are lazy or not as smart as people who sit up straight.

"Your body affects how you think. Your actions are based on what you think. And how you act affects what will happen to you. Let your body know you're strong and worthy, and you'll feel better about yourself.

2. Keep your head straight and your chin in the right place.

A level head is a sign of a confident, honest, and capable person. It could also make your voice sound fuller and look like you're looking people in the eye. With your head bowed and your eyes on the floor, you look uncertain, weak, submissive, and maybe even guilty of something.

3. Walk the walk.

As soon as you walk into a room with poise and confidence, people know you are someone important. Having a good balance is the first step to walking well. Keep your rib cage high and your chin up to walk confidently.

Keep your weight on the balls of your feet, and think tall and light. Don't get comfortable with each step. Keep your pace even and walk in a natural and relaxed way. People who walk with power move their arms more and take longer steps.

Keep hands visible.

Don't have both of your hands in your pockets. It makes you look uninterested, bored, indecisive, and sometimes nervous. Using one hand is fine if the other is making a sign. Keeping your hands open and palms up shows you are honest and ready to connect with others.

"Pockets are the killers of relationships. When people can see your hands, they feel more comfortable around you and are more likely to become your friend. Keep your hands out of your pockets when you walk into a room or wait to meet someone."

Look them in the eyes.

Your eyes are strong, silent tools because you can choose how to use them, and they do many things independently. When you meet someone for the first time, it's nice to look them in the eyes for a few seconds, but it's rude to look at them and stare. Short contact is fine, but looking at someone for long periods is seen as hostile or dangerous.

It's just as powerful to not look at someone. You might look away and stop making eye contact with the other person to let them know you are ready to end the chat or that they are talking too much. Not making eye contact with someone you just met is also a sign of low self-esteem or lack of trust in yourself. Between 40 and 60% of the time, eye contact should be made in the right places.

Use your face to make your message clearer.

When you talk or connect with someone, your face is the centre of attention, so its moves and expressions have a bigger effect. The face is a way to show how you're feeling and how you're feeling about something. It's also important for controlling and guiding a conversation. Once you've started talking to someone, your facial emotions can either make them want to talk to you more or stop them from doing so.

On the other hand, if you show too much emotion, it can hurt your trustworthiness. If you want to seem more authoritative, move and talk less. This is especially true if most people in the room are men. When you look cool and in charge, you look stronger.

Smiling is a strong and positive way to show that you are likeable and friendly without saying anything. When you first meet someone, it's especially important to smile because it shows that you're interested in them. Conversely, women should know that laughing too much at work can make them look less trustworthy.

A smile can help people get along better, fix problems, or stop fights. It lets the other person know that they can trust you."

Give them a strong grip.

A handshake can make people trust each other more in just a few seconds, and you should never underestimate its power. In the Western world, the handshake is the only accepted way to touch someone for the first time when doing business. Even with handshakes, the "basic" can be done in many ways.

If you want to make a good impression and show confidence, the most important thing to remember is to clasp the other person's hand tightly when you shake hands. When you feel their muscles getting tighter, stop.

"Handshakes are a good way to communicate without words. It is a form of engaging body language that shows how the other person sees the world, himself or herself, and you. It is a very important, but often unintentional, part of making a first impression and leaving a message.

"The Power of Handshaking" by Robert E. Brown and Dorothea Johnson.

Make your voice sound reliable and expert.

Voice is a big part of unconscious cues and actions that you send and receive. Most people don't know or understand how their voice affects what they don't say. Before meeting someone in person for the first time, you probably have talked to them on the phone. So, they can only judge you based on one thing: the way you sound.

So, you must have the right voice picture. Talk loudly and clearly. Don't mumble. Don't use filler words or words that aren't correct. Don't sound unsure of what you're saying, and don't apologize too much.

Use motions to get your point across.

If you want to look relaxed and natural, your body language needs to start talking as soon as you speak. Don't think about what you're doing with your hands; they should look normal and back up what you're saying. People pay attention when you use your hands.

Spence Kelly, a professor at Colgate University, says that they make people pay attention to how speech sounds. Use them rarely, but when it matters. Moving your hands too much or too far can be annoying and take away from what you are saying.

I like it when your gestures don't go above the top of your chest or below the bottom of your waist. But some people who study body language think that the power area goes all the way up to your face.

The Induction

Classical induction is a technique used to induce a hypnotic trance state in a person, often employed in the context of hypnotherapy and hypnosis conducted by a qualified professional. The main objectives of this technique are to relax both body and mind, concentrate attention and prepare the mind to accept suggestions.

Before starting the induction process, you must create a quiet, distraction-free environment and get comfortable.

It is essential to emphasize that each individual may respond differently to hypnotic induction, therefore approaching the person's specific reactions and needs.

Some of the most common induction hypnotic techniques are listed below:

Reverse Counting Induction: In this technique, the hypnotherapist guides the individual to count backwards, creating a feeling of relaxation and increasing concentration.

Staircase Induction: Here, the individual imagines descending a staircase, with the steps representing increasingly deeper trance states.

Wave Induction: The hypnotherapist guides the individual to imagine being lulled by soothing waves, thus promoting relaxation.

Gaze Induction: This technique involves the individual focusing on a specific object or point, such as a pendulum or light, to induce a trance state.

Breathing Induction: The individual is guided to focus on their breathing, creating a feeling of calm and relaxation.

Hand Induction: Here, the individual is guided to imagine their hands sticking together or becoming heavy, thus inducing relaxation.

Induction of muscle contraction and relaxation: The individual is guided to contract and relax their muscles, generating a sense of relaxation and reduction of tension.

Visualization Induction: The individual is led through a guided visualization, such as imagining a relaxing place or a pleasant experience.

Number induction: The hypnotherapist may use the "counting up" technique, in which the individual is guided to imagine that they are counting in a specific way.

Magnetic Hand Induction: Here, the individual is guided to imagine that their hands are like magnets attracting each other, creating a feeling of relaxation and focus.

These are just some of the hypnotic induction techniques available, and the therapist will choose the one that best suits the patient based on his needs and responses during the session. Classical induction is an invaluable tool within hypnotherapy, contributing to relaxation and facilitating the desired change process in the subconscious mind.

The choice of induction techniques in hypnosis depends on the individual's preferences and responses. A trained hypnotic therapist can tailor techniques to fit a person's specific needs and create an effective trance state.

The use of suggestions is a crucial element of hypnosis and self-hypnosis, as suggestions are positive statements or phrases introduced when the mind is in a hypnotic trance or deep relaxation. Suggestions aim to influence the subconscious and promote positive changes in thoughts, emotions and behaviours.

To get effective results with suggestions, it is important to follow a few guidelines:

Positive and specific wording: Suggestions should be worded positively, avoiding negative or ambiguous terms. For example, instead of saying, "You won't be anxious anymore," you can say, "You feel calm and peaceful."

Present tense: Suggestions should be expressed in the present tense, suggesting this is already happening. This helps the subconscious integrate the idea as a current reality. For example, "Every day, I feel more and more confident in myself."

First-person: It is advisable to use the first person in suggestions. This helps personalize the statement and create a deeper connection between the individual and the statement. For example, "I am full of confidence and positivity."

Specificity: Be specific in your suggestions rather than adopting vague statements. For example, instead of saying, "I'm good at handling stress," you can say, "Whenever I'm in a stressful situation, I stay calm and focused."

Repetition: Repeat the suggestions several times during the hypnosis session. Repetition helps reinforce the message in the subconscious, allowing for better assimilation of the affirmations. Well-formulated and carefully delivered suggestions can be a powerful tool in fostering positive changes in the subconscious mind and helping people achieve their goals and improve their mental and emotional well-being.

Adding emotion, vivid imagery, and engaging the senses to suggestions can greatly amplify their impact on the subconscious. Here are some additional guidelines to make suggestions even more effective:

Emotion and feeling: Suggestions expressed with deep emotion tend to have a more lasting impact. For example, "I feel great joy as I release my fears" adds an emotional element to the suggestion.

Vivid and detailed images: Use detailed and vivid descriptions in your suggestions. This helps the subconscious mind visualize the experience as if it were real. For example, "I see myself achieving my goals with ease" creates a clear picture.

Involve multiple senses: Try to involve all the senses in your suggestions. For example, "I feel the sensation of calm spreading through my body like a warm light" involves the sense of touch and the concept of calm.

Preparation: Before introducing the suggestions, ensure you are in deep relaxation and inner concentration. This helps create a greater openness to suggestions.

Time and Repetition: Suggestions must be fully integrated into the subconscious. Repeat hypnosis sessions with the same suggestions over an extended period to achieve lasting results.

Individual Variability: Consider the effectiveness of suggestions, motivation, suggestibility, and cooperation. An experienced practitioner can help tailor suggestions to each individual's needs and maximize positive results.

Suggestions can be a powerful tool for promoting positive changes in the subconscious mind and mental and emotional well-being.

Find Out How To Stop Having Negative Thoughts

Chapter 3.2: Gaining Reintegration

Dissociation interferes with our ability to feel, perceive bodily sensations, and form judgments about the outside world or oneself. This is a regular occurrence for people who have had a traumatic event or who are depressed or anxious. Individuals who experience dissociation frequently feel as though they are not in the actual world and fear that they are insane or that they have a terminal illness. Interacting with others becomes almost impossible, and the ensuing extreme anxiety may finally materialize as a disorder known as social phobia.

The experience of dissociation may differ from person to person depending on the conditions that preceded it. However, the following are some prevalent ideas and feelings associated with the state of dissociation:

- Everything seems surreal.
- A feeling of isolation from the outside world

A veil of grey that blocked their vision

As if your head were covered with a veil

The global speed of life is notably faster than the norm.

- Perplexity
- The terrible feeling that you can't handle the circumstance
- You don't have self-confidence
- Other people experience happiness, but not you.
- Serious anxiety

Feeling like there's someone against you at all times

● The feeling that others talk about you all the time

These are just a few of the emotions that dissociation can elicit. Eventually, the sufferer may start to feel that to reintegrate into reality, they must turn their attention inward. They are watchful of themselves, searching for any hint that the world they know is returning. Naturally, the symptoms worsen the more inwardly focused and anxious people become.

Cognitive behavioural therapy may prove to be beneficial for individuals who are experiencing difficulties in overcoming feelings of dissociation, especially when severe trauma is the underlying cause. When combined with the support and understanding of a medical expert, self-help techniques can help people who suffer dissociation due to stress and anxiety overcome their feelings.

Remember that nothing has changed fundamentally in the world; everything has changed only in your viewpoint about the people and things around you, and these are just passing thoughts and feelings you are going through right now. You will again see things as you did in the past after overcoming and vanquishing whatever is causing the dissociation sensations. It's important for those experiencing dissociative emotions as a result of depression and anxiety to remember that these experiences are just feelings and that they will eventually pass. Stop thinking about them after you try to accept that they are here to stay for a while. It's important to stop obsessing over them and wondering when they will depart. Once you lose interest in your feelings and stop thinking about them all the time, you might be surprised at how quickly the world goes back to being the one you knew. Since letting go of your dread of the situation is the only way to start the healing process, you must embrace your feelings and any thoughts that may occur to you during this time.

Getting Past Uncertainty in Chapter 3.3

Naturally, if you don't doubt it, overcoming scepticism is simple. All of us, though, harbour some doubts about our ability to succeed whenever we attempt something new. Almost everyone has uncertainty of some kind at some point in their lives. Take the science domain as an example. Do you think that if people had not initially questioned the presumptions, none of the scientific advancements that have been accomplished would have been possible? Assume that you are considering starting a novel project or a commercial endeavour. Do you have complete confidence that it will succeed? There is always some doubt and perhaps even anxiety in the beginning.

You can't let your doubts deter you from achieving your ultimate goal. It is a simple explanation. The danger of failing must be accepted since it is the only way to overcome self-doubt. Go for it with all your might, but don't make snap decisions. You won't get into the water without the appropriate protection, so don't worry. You're going to analyze every possible consequence of your situation thoroughly, and you're going to be accepting of whatever the outcome turns out to be. The secret to effectively navigating uncertainty is this. You will succeed if you can get the courage to give it everything you've got.

It is the believers who fight the forces of scepticism. Develop an optimistic outlook and confidence in your ability to accomplish your objectives. Remember that you can only succeed at your goals if you have faith in your ability to do so; if you have faith in your incapacity, you will likewise fail. You must discipline yourself to stop thinking negatively since your thoughts can create the reality you experience. In the same spirit, you should never trust the advice of those out to get you, who enjoy planting doubt in your thoughts, and who are wolves in sheep's clothing. Always surround yourself with positive thinkers and people with a positive outlook on life. You want to be among folks who are like them.

When something goes wrong

You most likely won't have the good fortune to never fail during your lifetime. You have to acknowledge that this is a normal part of life. When you fail, doubt creeps into your head and makes it harder to summon the confidence you had earlier in the process. These are the times. No matter how discouraged you are by past failures, you cannot back out of your commitment. Should you experience a setback, it should only make you more determined to try again and accomplish your goal. Develop the ability to train your thoughts to increase your confidence and self-control and achieve this.

You may eliminate self-doubt by increasing your confidence, and before you know it, you'll be back to getting the desired outcomes.

Sufficient scepticism

It is crucial to remember that uncertainty is always a good thing when it comes to growing older or becoming a better person. However, you should use your mental toughness reserves to overcome it when it starts to contribute to your sadness and inactivity or when it feels like an insurmountable obstacle to getting where you're going. You must strengthen your will to succeed at all costs and seek to minimize self-doubt to design a life that brings you great satisfaction.

You might succeed despite your hesitation or perhaps precisely because of it. Alternatively, you may have little choice except to accept the worst-case scenario and give in to the inevitable. If this happens, just do a U-turn, start your engine again, and start travelling your new route from the start. Before your doubts can conquer you, conquer them.

Providing Incentives for Every Goal Attained

Setting targets and rewarding yourself makes it much easier to stay focused and motivated, even though creating goals could be challenging! If you make this deal with yourself, you will achieve your objectives!

While not everyone approaches goal-setting similarly, everyone follows a similar procedure while making lists. A must-watch movie list, must-buy list, must-read book list, or to-do list might be on it. These milestones can be continuous, annual, monthly, bimonthly, or daily. Each of them affects your life in some way.

Occasionally, these goals are straightforward. Empty the trash? Verify! Does the dishwasher need to be loaded? Completed! Some goals, nevertheless, are quite difficult to accomplish, like the lifelong goal of adopting a better lifestyle. Why is this the case? The absence of an immediate reward is a primary factor contributing to the difficulty of these long-term objectives. It's discouraging to exercise, consume a nutritious diet for months, and notice minimal physical transformation. That's why it's equally crucial to recognize and celebrate minor victories.

Reaching a lesser goal doesn't always require a complicated or costly reward. For instance, it wouldn't be possible to wake up one day and give up Coke forever, even if that was your goal. It is more sensible to begin with small steps. A two-week aim might be your shorter-term target; if you can maintain it, you could arrange a reward. Perhaps the benefit is that the funds that would have been spent on drinks can now be saved for new clothes. You'll have more money for new clothes the longer you abstain from soda. That's how easy it is!

All you have to do is decide on a positive consequence for reaching a certain, attainable goal. Ensure you honour your promises to yourself and treat yourself with genuine pleasure. Your goals ought to be challenging but doable. Pushing yourself to perform better on the current target is the aim.

Try to devise a reasonable objective for yourself at the end of this chapter and put it in writing. You should say something like this: "I (your name) recognize that I am always working on myself and my self-esteem. I promise to stay committed to these goals and, in turn, reward myself when I meet a goal. I won't feel guilty about my reward. I promise to practice self-care for the term of this contract, which is ____ months."

Proceed by decomposing the objectives into more manageable steps and documenting them, as previously mentioned. Even easier would be to create a synopsis for each aim that has been split down. For instance, your summary can be "no soda" if you want to reduce your soda use. Put it on sticky notes and affix them to key locations to easily see them.

Life Is Too Challenging

Success should be determined more by the challenges one has surmounted than by the place one has attained. –Booker T. Washington

The simplest years of your life are behind you now, so you will either have to change or live a horrible existence for the remainder of it. Although that is the most direct way to phrase everything in this chapter, it seems too clear-cut. But how often have you uttered or thought something along those lines? Life is just too difficult. It's easy for everyone else. Why do my parents focus on such little things and make my life difficult?

Since we have all said it at some point, it is simpler to account for those who have never done so. I have said that even as an adult. Every time, my mother reminds me that some are far worse off than me.

But Mom, we're not talking about them!

I want to talk about why you feel that way in this chapter. What is it about being a teenager that makes it so hard? Why does it seem like everything you do causes you to go higher and higher? You'll learn that despite your best efforts, you will inevitably encounter difficulties, tension, worry, and all of the above. Although it's all a part of the process, it makes accepting and going beyond setbacks very difficult.

It will be satisfying to realize and accept that life is now in hard mode since it will at least make the challenging aspects more bearable so you can still enjoy life. Let's begin with what is bothering you and making your path incredibly challenging.

The Challenges of Adolescence

In all seriousness, though, I hope you realize that not everyone has an easy life—even teenagers. If you didn't know, I strongly advise you to take a moment to see things from a different angle by stepping outside your world. Some truly have it worse off than you. Additionally, I would advise you to listen to your parents when they say they understand—because they do. Try to acknowledge that they were teenagers once, even if you don't understand this concept immediately.

Now, though, let's turn the attention back to you because adolescence seems like the worst time of life for a few frequent reasons.

You find yourself caught between a child and an adult.

You've already lived through the easiest years of your life, and you know that the struggle will only intensify once you're independent. The fact that it appears like no one else understands how to handle you only makes it worse. Are you still a little child in need of continual supervision? Are you reaching adulthood and needing more responsibilities?

Some parents are doing their hardest because they truly don't know what to do, and raising a teenager is very hard. Even when it seems they're not giving it their all, they are. Because they can't fully accept the idea that you're growing up, some go too far, which is why some will spoil you, and others expect you to be prepared to move out when you're eighteen.

Not to mention that you're bridging that gap while dealing with whatever you want to be carefree and innocent, but you also know that you must take approaching adulthood seriously.

You have no idea how to handle all the changes happening to you.

Not only are you experiencing bodily changes at an astounding rate, but you also have new hormones to cope with, which will provide your own set of challenges, and no one is advising you on how to handle them!

It feels so hard since these grownups should know how to handle these problems if they were teenagers once.

Is "accepting that this is all part of the ride of life" one of the tiniest responses to how to handle adolescence? We know how to handle it. Indeed, but that is the case. This is a part of the experience, and each voyage will be as distinct as the individual taking it.

Your parents give you endless lectures about everything.

Every action you take seems like an opportunity for your parents to impart wisdom to you. Parents are attempting to mould you into a healthy, functioning adult by imparting their knowledge and lessons learnt during their adolescent years. However, it sounds more like nagging and lecturing than it does.

It can be quite draining to feel like they are constantly bugging you about everything you've done, are, and will do. When you combine this with the hormones and emotions that are out of balance due to your body changing, it can eventually result in some trying moments and strained relationships with your parents.

It should be clear to you already what you want to accomplish in life.

After going through these things, all of a sudden, everyone is asking you what you want to do with your life. It seems like everyone starts talking to you as soon as you become a teenager about careers, colleges, and how to prepare for them.

You hardly know what you want to do when you're a teenager, much less what you want to do in five years. Then, recruiters, guest lecturers, and other people attempt to sway you. Anyone who experiences it may feel as though they are always being tugged in different directions, which raises tension and anxiety levels to a dangerously high degree.

You're Going Through Heartbreaks and Your First Real Relationships.

Even while there are relationships in those early years, you know they aren't very meaningful. One day, you could ask someone out before classes start, and you would be declared enemies by lunchtime. Everything moves too fast to be worth mentioning.

But things change when you reach adolescence. The influence of these associations increases along with the intensity of the feelings. Is it because you consider this other person a part of your future because you have so many questions about your adult life and future? Are you experiencing new emotions and hormones as a result? Or is it the case that you still lack a true perspective of what the world looks like?

You see this individual as someone who will stick around long after you're a teenager, regardless of the reason. This will be painful when the relationship ends since it begins to give you the first real feelings of permanence with someone.

There's a recent drama involving your pals.

Your buddy relationships will undoubtedly be more dramatic than they were previously, even though your sexual interactions might not be as tumultuous. You might be best friends one day, but you see them chatting to someone you don't like. You're enemies by the next morning. But after a week, you get back together and continue as if nothing had occurred.

When you're in a relationship, observing someone outside of it becomes even more confusing. Even though your parents and other adults will undoubtedly tell you it's not a big problem, to you, it is. That's assuming you make up with the other person; otherwise, it's distracting and stressful. Bullying and other issues may arise if the situation is not handled and the wedge widens.

Acknowledging Self-Compassion

Practising self-kindness is a step on the route to self-love. Let's explore what it means to be kind to yourself. Loving oneself is being kind to yourself. Treating oneself with compassion, warmth, and understanding is known as self-kindness. It entails treating yourself with the same respect and consideration as a close friend or loved one. Being kind and compassionate to oneself, particularly under trying or painful circumstances, entails supporting, caring, and forgiving yourself. It focuses on providing yourself with support, comfort, and encouragement.

THE NEED FOR SELF-KINDNESS

It entails nurturing a good and encouraging connection by being kind, empathetic, and gentle with yourself. Self-kindness practices are crucial for our general wellbeing and pleasure in today's hectic and demanding world, where external expectations and pressures can be unbearable.

Regarding self-acceptance and self-love, self-kindness is crucial. You recognize and respect your intrinsic worth and value as a human being when you treat yourself with kindness. When you practice self-kindness, you may accept your inadequacies with compassion and understanding rather than criticizing them.

Additionally essential to stress management and resilience building is self-kindness. We all have hardships, disappointments, and terrible situations in life, which can be difficult. Self-kindness serves as a cushion, providing consolation and comfort during these times. It enables you to accept yourself for who you are and realize that you are doing your best. By being kind to yourself, you release unneeded pressure off yourself and make room for recovery, development, and rejuvenation.

Furthermore, self-kindness is beneficial to your mental and emotional health. Your internal self-care practices significantly influence your thoughts, feelings, and general state of mind. Thinking critically or judgmentally about yourself limits your potential and reinforces negative thoughts. Conversely, self-kindness cultivates an encouraging and constructive internal conversation. You can cultivate a positive and powerful mindset that supports resilience and self-confidence by keeping an eye on your self-talk and substituting positive and supportive statements for self-criticism.

Physical wellbeing is directly associated with self-kindness as well. By treating your body with respect and compassion, you may prioritize self-care and create healthy behaviours. It entails paying close attention to and listening to your body's requirements. Self-kindness guides decisions that promote your physical wellbeing, such as exercising frequently or obtaining the right medical attention.

Moreover, practising self-kindness improves your interactions with other people. You become more aware of your wants and feelings when treating yourself with care. You can connect and speak with people from a place of sincerity and empathy when you have self-awareness. You may create a culture of compassion and understanding by practising self-kindness and inspiring and motivating others to do the same.

Dispelling Untruths Regarding Self-Kindness

Notwithstanding the manifold advantages and significance of self-kindness, several myths and misunderstandings may prevent people from completely adopting this practice. Let's examine some widespread misconceptions about self-kindness:

Myth 1: Self-indulgence equals self-kindness

There is a misconception that self-indulgence and self-kindness are synonymous. On the other hand, excessive self-focus or putting your own needs ahead of others are not characteristics of self-kindness. It's about striking a balance between taking care of yourself and others, realizing that taking care of yourself enables you to participate more fully and genuinely in your obligations and relationships.

Let's use Mandy as an example. Mandy gives her ageing parents her whole attention. Taking care of their needs, scheduling their doctor's visits, and ensuring they have all they need to occupy most of their time. Mandy is constantly tired and stressed out, and she hardly ever takes time for herself.

Mandy feels that caring for herself would be indulgent or selfish in this situation. She worries that she could be abandoning her parental duties by putting her health first. The misunderstanding that self-kindness equates to self-indulgence is the foundation of this notion.

However, Mandy's lack of self-compassion negatively impacts her physical, mental, and emotional well-being. She begins to feel bitter, exhausted, and incapable of giving her parents the kind of care she wants to give them. Mandy understands that putting off her needs makes it harder for her to provide good care for others.

Through a change of viewpoint, Mandy begins to see that self-kindness is not selfish but crucial to her general well-being and the care she gives. She understands she is just as worthy of love, kindness, and self-care as her parents.

Mandy begins to practice self-compassion in tiny ways. She establishes limits for herself by planning regular self-care time, using that time to relax and partake in enjoyable activities. She goes to yoga twice a week, grabs coffee with friends, or strolls through the outdoors at her own pace. She feels refreshed and reenergized after engaging in these self-care activities.

Mandy discovers that practising self-kindness helps her parents as much as she does. During their exchanges, she grows more present, patient, and kind. Mandy discovers she has more vitality, compassion, and fortitude to give her parents when she attends to her needs.

You can see that self-kindness is not the same as self-indulgence or selfishness by looking at Mandy's example. It is crucial to preserving general wellbeing and having the capacity to successfully support others. Understanding and meeting your needs improves your capacity to provide for others and helps you live a more contented and balanced life. Being self-kind does not mean forgetting your duties; it means striking a balance that enables you to provide genuine, loving care for yourself and others.

Myth No. 2: Being Self-Kind is Weakness

Some might interpret self-kindness as a sign of fragility or vulnerability. They think facing challenges head-on and being hard on oneself is a more honourable strategy. But self-kindness is an expression of endurance and strength, not of weakness. It takes guts to accept your frailties, own your limitations, and be kind to yourself when faced with difficulties.

Let's discuss Carter as an example. As an accomplished project manager, Carter has always taken great satisfaction in his unwavering dedication and strong work ethic. He feels that the secret to success is constantly pushing himself, and showing self-kindness is a sign of weakness. Carter is harsh with himself and always holds himself to a high level.

Carter had a significant setback at work one day. When a project he was leading didn't turn out as he had hoped, he felt disappointed and guilty about himself. Carter used to criticize himself for the setback since he saw it as a reflection of his shortcomings.

But Carter chooses to tackle the matter differently this time. Taking a step back, he sees the negative consequences of his critical thinking. He understands that pushing himself too hard without showing self-compassion is unsustainable and frequently results in burnout and a decline in motivation.

Carter decides to practice self-kindness in light of his newfound insight. Rather than criticizing himself for the failure, he accepts that mistakes happen and that he is human. He tells himself that failures are chances for development and education. Carter ponders what went wrong for a while. Instead of concentrating on his errors, he now concentrates on the lessons he has learned and the actions he can do to improve.

Carter starts to see improvements in his performance and general wellbeing as he embraces self-kindness. He discovers that being kind and sympathetic to himself increases his drive, grit, and capacity for problem-solving. Through the practice of self-kindness, Carter has improved his ability to overcome obstacles and adjust to changing circumstances.

By looking at Carter's example, you may see that self-kindness is a sign of strength and resilience rather than weakness. You may overcome obstacles, grow from your errors, and eventually achieve more success and wellbeing when you practice self-kindness. Being compassionate toward yourself and accepting your humanity requires bravery, but when you do, you build a foundation of strength and resiliency that benefits every aspect of your life.

Chapter 15: Leaning in and accepting vulnerability: It's okay to cry.

Vulnerability may accompany the person on a perpetual emotional roller coaster as they overcome unrequited love. This fifteenth chapter will discuss the significance of accepting vulnerability as a normal component of the emotional healing process. Tears are not a sign of weakness; they are a means of emotional release and expression that help the person advance toward a deeper understanding of themselves and further personal development.

Deconstructing susceptibility

Vulnerability has always been stigmatized by society, which sees it as a sign of weakness. Notwithstanding, susceptibility is an intrinsic aspect of the human condition and an indication of genuineness and emotional bonding. Vulnerability allows the person to have a deeper connection with themselves and others.

sobbing as a way to release emotions

Weeping is an outlet for pent-up feelings, particularly heartache and psychological suffering. Letting yourself cry is a technique to heal emotional wounds and communicate what cannot be spoken via words.

Acknowledging bravery in being vulnerable

Taking on vulnerability calls for bravery. Facing and expressing one's feelings, especially when painful or difficult to handle, takes courage. Realizing that crying is a display of emotional power rather than weakness requires first acknowledging the bravery in vulnerability.

The efficaciousness of introspection

Being vulnerable can lead to introspection and self-discovery. The person can explore his deepest feelings and desires by letting himself be exposed.

Embracing feelings for what they are

Accepting emotions for what they are, without condemning or suppressing them, is what it means to embrace vulnerability. It's letting go of guilt and allowing yourself to feel depressed, angry, or frustrated. Respecting and being compassionate toward oneself involves accepting one's emotions.

The relationship between sensitivity and compassion

Being vulnerable can increase empathy for both oneself and other people. The act of being vulnerable enables one another, hence fortifying emotional bonds between them.

The value of emotional assistance

While accepting vulnerability, getting emotional support from friends, family, or experts can be a great resource for assistance.

Talking to others about the experience can help you feel less alone and more at ease while you work toward emotional recovery.

Being vulnerable is a liberating act.

Accepting your vulnerability may be a freeing experience. It involves letting go of the desire to keep up a strong front and permitting yourself to be real with people and yourself. It's realizing that vulnerability is normal and does not lessen your worth or value.

The value of expressing emotions

Emotional wellbeing depends on having appropriate emotional expression. Crying is one of the most organic and efficient ways to express emotions; it allows feelings to come out and be processed.

Being vulnerable can lead to healing.

Emotional healing may be attainable via vulnerability. Being vulnerable can heal emotional wounds and release stored emotional tensions.

putting up with flaws

Accepting one's imperfection is a prerequisite for embracing vulnerability. It is realizing that none of us are immune to emotional suffering and are susceptible to weaknesses. To accept imperfection is to be self-pitying and humble.

Resilience's function

When it comes to accepting vulnerability, emotional resilience is an invaluable asset. It is the capacity to adjust and bounce back from emotional setbacks. Being resilient enables one to grow from challenging circumstances and advance more confidently.

fostering a closer bond with oneself

Being vulnerable might be a chance to develop a more intimate, understanding relationship with oneself. The person can listen to her emotional needs and take loving, compassionate care of himself by letting himself be vulnerable.

In conclusion, crying is a human expression.

It is a sign of humanity and honesty to embrace vulnerability and let oneself cry. It is acknowledging that every one of us is an emotional being capable of profoundly impacting experiences and changes.

The person can break free from the belief that crying indicates weakness in this chapter. Instead, he realizes that sobbing is a brave act that allows one to express emotions when confronted with emotional challenges.

Gain a deeper understanding of themselves by accepting their vulnerability. It is an act of self-love and authenticity that offers a fresh viewpoint on the road to a happier, more fulfilling existence and the process of emotional recovery.

workout routine

Regular exercise raises dopamine levels and energy expenditure, which can help with attention.

Food Is Essential

Observe good nutrition. Meals high in complex carbohydrates and omega-3 fatty acids may improve brain function.

Set attainable objectives.

Divide your objectives into doable phases. Reward minor accomplishments along the road to maintain your motivation.

Acknowledge Your Interests

Use your hobbies to help you focus your hyperfocus. Take full advantage of your passions in painting, music, or any other activity.

Create a Network of Support

Tell the people you care about about your experience managing ADHD. Inform them about your needs and difficulties, and rely on their assistance when you require it.

Overcome obstacles.

ADHD comes with its share of challenges. Consider your errors as opportunities to improve rather than as places to wallow in regret.

Employment Opportunities

Seek occupations that fit your interests and skill set. Successful people with ADHD frequently succeed in technology, business, and the arts.

Drugs

Medication could be useful if advised. Talk carefully with your healthcare practitioner about the best type and dosage for you.

Reach your objectives.

Defend your interests. Be clear about your expectations for both the classroom and the workplace. Ask for changes if needed.

Continue to be Happy

Keep a cheerful outlook. On this path, self-acceptance and self-compassion are essential.

Continuous Training

Learn more about ADHD. Your ability to manage your illness will improve with more understanding of it.

Remember that accepting your individuality is the key to beating ADHD. Your particular brain structure may contribute to extraordinary creativity and success. You can use your ADHD as a superpower and apply it to your path to success and fulfilment if you have the correct techniques and support.

7. Quality of Sleep and Restoring Energy

The Obstacle:

Insufficient sleep can cause energy disruption and cognitive impairment.

The Resolution:

- Sleep Prioritization:

- Make sure you get enough good sleep. The ideal amount of sleep for physical and mental recovery is seven to nine hours each night. More rested and energized.

- Regular Sleep Schedule:

- Keep a regular sleep routine. Aids in regulating your circadian cycle, which enhances the quality of your sleep.

8. Awareness and Rejuvenation of Energy

The Obstacle:

Even after physical recovery, mental exhaustion might linger.

The Resolution:

- Conscious Activities:

- Include mindfulness exercises in your daily routine. Methods like deep breathing, meditation, or mindfulness exercises can assist in reviving your Energy and clearing mental weariness.

- Intentional Breathing Pauses:

- Take brief, deliberate breaths. Take a few minutes to focus yourself and release mental tension by concentrating on your breathing. This exercise improves focus and clarity.

9. Impacts of the Environment and Society on Energy

The Obstacle:

Ignoring how the environment and social interactions affect one's energy levels.

The Resolution:

- Satisfying Social Exchanges:

- Be in the company of uplifting social encounters. Talking to friends or coworkerswho are encouraging can make you feel more energized. On the other hand, limit your exposure to unfavourable influences that could sap your vitality.

- Streamlining Work Area:

- Make the most of the Energy in your office. Make sure there is adequate lighting, cosy seating, and clutter-free space. These elements support an upbeat and stimulating work environment.

10. Continuous Evaluation and Modification

The Obstacle:

Energy management is a dynamic process therefore tactics can need to be modified.

The Resolution:

- Regular Evaluation:

- Evaluate the success of your energy management tactics regularly. Consider your strengths and areas for improvement. Adapt your strategy in light of evolving situations and your understanding.

- Adaptability & Flexibility:

- Be willing to modify your schedule as needed. Because life is dynamic, unforeseen circumstances could affect your energy management strategy. As your daily schedule changes, make the necessary adjustments while keeping energy optimization in mind.

In summary:

Interactions between the mental, emotional, and physical aspects affecting your everyday functioning are effective energy management. You may maximize your energy levels and improve overall productivity by scheduling tasks around your natural energy peaks, taking breaks, prioritising sleep, and adopting mindful practices. Remember that energy management is a unique path that requires constant self-reflection and modification. May your dedication to recognizing and utilizing your Energy result in long-term optimal performance, increased well-being, and a satisfying work-life equilibrium.

www.ingramcontent.com/pod-product-compliance
Lightning Source LLC
Chambersburg PA
CBHW052150110526
44591CB00012B/1919